Original title:
Joy Wrapped in Pine and Snow

Copyright © 2024 Creative Arts Management OÜ
All rights reserved.

Author: Ronan Whitfield
ISBN HARDBACK: 978-9916-90-890-7
ISBN PAPERBACK: 978-9916-90-891-4

Enchanted Snowfall Beneath Green Canopies

Snowflakes dance like silly sprites,
Under pines in festive sights.
Fluffy hats on trees so tall,
Nature's joke, we love it all.

Squirrels skate on icy shelves,
Searching for their hidden elves.
Winter chuckles, birds take flight,
Chirping stories through the night.

Comfort in Frosty Embraces

Cocoa mugs with marshmallow clouds,
Snowmen laugh in frosty crowds.
A penguin slips, a soft 'whoops',
While hot air balloons suit groups.

Snuggled close in knitted wraps,
Laughter echoes, playful claps.
Ice cream cones, oh icy treats,
With silly hats and frosty feats.

Glimmering Pines and Dazzling Eves

Pine cones twinkle like lost stars,
Right next to sleds and candy cars.
Elks in glitter, prancing proud,
Snowball toss, the giggles loud.

Footprints lead to secret dens,
Where raccoons play with silly pens.
Frosty nights with stories bright,
Carry on till morning light.

Nature's Tapestry of Bliss

The trees wear crowns of snowy lace,
While squirrels crack nuts at a fervent pace.
Lights twinkle on the frozen ground,
As frosty giggles swirl all around.

The winds sing tunes of shivering glee,
While owls hoot jokes in harmony.
A bear in boots slides with grace,
Forgetting his lunch in this wild space.

The Cheer of Frosted Pines

Pines stand tall in fluffy white hats,
As moose dance awkwardly like acrobats.
Snowballs fly and laughter spreads,
While mice plan parties in their warm beds.

With each crackle of winter's mirth,
The world spins round, a comic rebirth.
Giggling winds weave tales of fun,
As snowflakes fall, one by one.

Luminescent Nights in the Woods

In the moonlight, deer prance and leap,
While raccoons steal snacks from a cozy heap.
Stars wink down at the silly scene,
As coyotes serenade the serene.

The chilly air buzzes with silly dreams,
While laughter spills in glittering streams.
Beneath the pines, a snowball fight,
Turns the dusk into a sheer delight.

Whispers of Winter's Embrace

In the chill where snowflakes prance,
Squirrels dance in a silly stance,
They slip and slide with laughter loud,
Bobbling round like a jolly crowd.

Hot cocoa spills on knitted gear,
While snowmen sport a scarf and a sneer,
Their carrot noses, quite a sight,
Attracting birds that chirp in delight.

Frost-Kissed Memories and Enchanted Woods

In the wood, squirrels perform,
Chasing snowflakes, oh, what a norm!
Branches wear crowns made of white,
They giggle and dance, pure delight.

Beneath the drifts, a rabbit pranks,
Hiding its stash from the snowy banks.
With every hop, the laughter flies,
A symphony played by furry spies.

Frosted Laughter in the Grove

In the grove where the chill is strong,
Funny critters all tag along,
They tumble 'round, then strike a pose,
With silly hats and frozen toes.

Frosty air carries each chuckling sound,
As winter's humor spins all around,
Under the trees, they share good cheer,
In this winter circus, oh-so-dear.

Echoes of Evergreen Bliss

Evergreen trees, dressed in white coats,
Whisper secrets in snowy notes,
Frisky rabbits hop in their glee,
As they chase their friends by the old oak tree.

A snowball fight breaks out at last,
With laughter echoing unsurpassed,
Snowflakes kiss cheeks, rosy and bright,
While winter's charm brings endless delight.

Sprigs of Delight Beneath Frost

Pine cones gather, a snoozy bunch,
Squirrels munch on a frosty brunch,
Giggles hide in the frosty air,
As fluffy friends play without a care.

Icicles dangle like candy canes,
Chasing each other in snowy lanes,
Frosty giggles abound and sway,
Making fun of the wintery play.

Luminous Skies Over Snow-Draped Pines

Stars twinkle like eyes in night,
Snowmen strut in pure delight.
One's nose is a carrot, oh so grand,
While another's hat flies off—how unplanned!

Pine trees sway in a gentle breeze,
Dressed in blankets that tease and freeze.
They whisper tales of snowy cheer,
As laughter echoes, loud and clear.

Whimsy in the Winter Wonderland

In the forest, laughter grows,
Thick as the snow, soft as a pose.
Mice in scarves scamper and play,
While owls chuckle at the ballet.

Icicles hang with shimmying glee,
They slide down branches, free as can be.
Every tree holds a secret grin,
Amongst winter's charm, let the fun begin!

The Smiles of Pinewood Trails

Pine cones scatter like tiny hats,
Wearing the frosty, fluffy spats.
Footprints lead to mischief, you bet,
Where snowball fights are not to forget.

Chirping birds sing silly tunes,
As flakes tumble down, like tiny-loons.
Everyone slips, giggles at show,
In winter's realm, where laughter flows.

Frosted Heartbeats in Quiet Pines

Under winter's blanket, giggles arise,
Snowflakes tickle noses, oh what a surprise!
Furry friends prance, with a hop and a leap,
While the world around slumbers, cozy and deep.

Icicles dangle like a jester's grin,
Chasing our shadows, let the fun begin!
We'll build a snowman, round as a ball,
With silly eyes made from pebbles, standing tall.

A Chorus of Chill and Cheer

Laughter erupts in the crisp, frozen air,
With snowball fights causing tousled hair.
Fluffy mittens thrown while sliding downhill,
Oh, what a sight, the thrill we can't still!

Frosted branches sway, like they're dancing to glee,
Squirrels search for acorns, all giggly and free.
The sound of our chuckles, a chorus so bright,
As we slide into winter, our hearts feel so light!

The Silvery Sigh of the Pine Forest

Pines whisper secrets in the frosty breeze,
While snowmen wave back with curious ease.
Skis on my feet, feeling clumsy, who knew?
Oh look! Here comes that tree, wearing snow as its shoe!

Round the frosted lagoon, we stomp and we play,
The echoing laughter makes winter's gray sway.
With each chilly breath, a puff of delight,
As the trees shake their heads in pure winter's spite!

Memories of Laughter in the Cold

The chill in the air is a chilly comedian,
With every loud giggle, feeling like a medium.
Hot cocoa cups clink like cheers in the frost,
Comparing silly stories of what was once lost.

Each flake that falls takes a jab at my hat,
As I stumble and tumble like a clumsy cat.
Huddled with friends, swapping jests of the day,
In this frozen wonderland, we play and we sway!

Frosty Vows to Celebrate

With mittens stuck on both our hands,
We made some vows in snowy lands.
A wedding cake of frosty flakes,
Who knew that love could leave such wakes?

The ring slipped off, it took a dive,
Into a mound where snowmen thrive.
But in this chill, we just can't frown,
With frozen smiles, we wear the crown!

Laughter Under a Blanket of Stars

When snowflakes dance like silly sprites,
We race the moon on frosty nights.
The laughter echoes from the trees,
While pinecones fall with playful ease.

Each twinkle light a giggle bright,
We stumble on the ice, what a sight!
With sleds that veer and friends that fall,
Our hearts are light, and we stand tall!

Pine Fragrance in the Crisp Air

The scent of pine and winter cheer,
An aroma strong, we hold so dear.
We try to sing, though voices crack,
As squirrels and birds just laugh at that!

Our noses red, we brave the cold,
While stories of snowmen are retold.
With gingerbread men that dance in glee,
It's a feast of fun, for you and me!

The Delicate Balance of Chill and Cheer

A snowball flies, it finds its mark,
Laughter spreads, a joyful spark.
With hot cocoa that spills and drips,
We sense the chill with giggly quips!

We dance around the frosty snow,
In lost boots and hats, we laugh and go.
The balance sways between warm and cold,
In moments like this, we're pure-hearted gold!

Boughs of Happiness Under a Frozen Sky

The branches hang low, a fluffy sight,
With squirrels in coats, they dart left and right.
A snowman rebels, with a carrot for flair,
While snowballs fly straight through the chilly air.

The wind whispers secrets, a giggle or two,
As penguins in mittens march past with a crew.
Each flake is a wink, a tickle of fun,
In a world made of laughter, let's all come undone.

Glimmers of Light in the Chill

Tiny lights sparkle like stars in the night,
As reflections dance wild, oh what a sight!
The hot cocoa's steaming, with marshmallows bold,
While carolers sing tunes, their voices all gold.

Frosty the snowman tries on a hat,
But it's just his old broom that keeps tipping flat.
With laughter and cheer, the cold can't subdue,
For warmth comes from smiles, and that's very true.

Snowflakes Dance on Pine Needles

The snowflakes are twirling, like dancers in glee,
Landing softly on branches, for all eyes to see.
A bird in a scarf, gives a chirpy hello,
While rabbits in boots hop around in the snow.

The pine cones are drawn in a jolly parade,
As squirrels put on shows, acorn masquerade.
With every soft crunch, the laughter does flow,
In this whimsical world where the cold winds blow.

A Harmony of Winter's Glow

The sunset's a canvas, with colors that sing,
As snowmen joke 'round about who's the king.
The trees wear their coats, a frosty ensemble,
While critters declare it a wintertime ramble.

A frozen pond sparkles, the skaters arrive,
With wobbly dances, oh, how they contrive!
They twirl with such flair, like they're on a show,
In this lighthearted ballet where giggles do flow.

The Cheerful Boughs Above

The branches sway with glee,
As squirrels plan their spree.
They bounce and leap, oh so spry,
Searching for nuts as they fly.

A bird lands and gives a squawk,
While rabbits dash and frolic, they talk.
With twinkling eyes they share a grin,
In this winter wonder, let the fun begin.

Sunbeams on Icy Branches

The sun peeks through with a playful wink,
Ice crystals shimmer, oh what a link!
The trees sparkle like stars on a stage,
Nature's own stand-up, setting the gauge.

A light-hearted breeze begins to tease,
Chasing snowflakes, swirling with ease.
They giggle and dance, a magical scene,
As shadows stretch long, so sleek and clean.

A Dance of Snowflakes and Light

Snowflakes twirl with a clap and a cheer,
They tumble and glide, oh what a sphere!
Each one a dancer, with style and flair,
Bowing and spinning, without a care.

Out comes the sun, with a warm embrace,
Melting some flakes, a game of chase.
With laughter so bright, and spirits so light,
The season's humor is pure delight.

Evergreen Echoes of Delight

The pines stand tall, their humor is sly,
Watching the antics of passerby.
With branches outstretched, they hold their breath,
As snowmen wobble, flirting with death.

A family tumbles, laughter's the sound,
In this frozen playground, joy knows no bound.
The echoes of giggles ripple through trees,
Nature's own chorus, a melody of ease.

Luminescence Among the Pines

The trees wear lights, oh what a sight,
A squirrel's dance makes spirits bright.
Snowballs fly, a cheeky throw,
As laughter echoes, all aglow.

Hot cocoa swirls, marshmallows hop,
Frosty faces, can't make them stop!
The branches sway, a festive cheer,
"Oops, there goes my hat!"—loud and clear.

Heartstrings Tied to Winter's Charm

Scarves wrapped tight, a funny fight,
With frozen toes, we take to flight.
Snowmen grinning, carrot noses,
Ah, Winter's chill, it just exposes.

Sleds that slide with silly cries,
Down the hill, oh how we fly!
Falling down, we roll in mirth,
Winter giggles, a joyful birth.

The Enchantment of Silver Haired Nights

Silver flakes twirl, a dizzy dance,
The moonlit glow gives us a chance.
Whispers of snow, tickle the trees,
And frosty noses say, "Oh, please!"

A howling wind joins in the song,
As little tots join, they can't go wrong.
Hot pies cooling on a windowsill,
"Keep your mittens!"—the air's a thrill!

Beneath the Pine's Embrace

Pine needles crunch, a rhythmic beat,
A snowball lands, oh what a treat!
A bear in a hat, what a strange sight,
Under the stars, everything's right.

Giggles and snorts, what a delight,
Tripping over each other, we take flight.
In this frosty wonderland we roam,
Each snowy flake feels just like home.

Merry Whispers in the Air

In a world where frosty flakes dance,
Squirrels in coats take a merry prance.
Snowmen wobble with carrot-nose grins,
While snowballs fly, oh, where to begin?

Chasing my mittens, they slip and slide,
With giggles echoing, I can't hide.
Paw prints trace tales of laughter and cheer,
As winter games draw everyone near.

Trails of Frosty Footprints

Boots crunch loud on the fluffy white,
Mapping the chaos, oh what a sight!
I slip and stumble, my balance in doubt,
But laughter erupts, that's what it's about!

Fluffy flakes fall like confetti from air,
On my nose, they land without a care.
Each step a dance, each laugh a thrill,
Frosty footprints lead to winter's goodwill.

Radiance in the Snowy Silence

Snow blankets the world like a fluffy rug,
Behind every tree, there's a squirrel to mug.
Whispers of laughter mix with the breeze,
As snowflakes tumble with graceful ease.

The world glistens like a giant cake,
I try to catch snow on my tongue with a shake.
Each sweet moment brings chuckles anew,
In this winter wonder, we'll make quite a crew!

Gleeful Shadows of Twilight

As day fades away, the snow starts to glow,
Shadowed figures dance through the wintery show.
With every tumble and joyful cheer,
The twilight giggles, it's perfectly clear.

Snowball fights turn into pure delight,
Frosty-haired friends join the playful fight.
With rosy cheeks and laughter that flies,
Twilight brings giggles beneath starlit skies.

Magical Moments in Evergreen

The squirrels all dance, in their furry attire,
Building snow forts, they never tire.
With pinecones as grenades, they throw and cheer,
Chasing each other without a single fear.

The trees start to shimmy, with a giggle or two,
As snowflakes descend, a soft frosty brew.
Branches are tickling, oh what a sight,
Nature's own party, everything feels right.

Embracing the Chill with Glee

Bundled up tight, like a present in wraps,
I slide on the ice, doing dazzling mishaps.
The dogs all are laughing, they gallop around,
While I'm there flopping, with no sense I found.

Hot cocoa in hand, but it's never quite hot,
I spill all my dreams, in a colorful pot.
Marshmallows float, like my hopes up so high,
While my socks fill with snow, oh my, oh my!

The Hushed Melody of Snowfall

The world is a blanket; all quiet, serene,
With snowmen conspiring, in hats they convene.
They gossip about winter, and chuckle with glee,
While I face plant in drifts, stuck like a tree.

In the distance, a snowball gets thrown with great care,
It lands on my head, oh, that's really unfair!
Underneath all the white, there's raucous delight,
As I shake off the snow, my laughter takes flight.

Charmed by Winter's Glow

Candles are twinkling, like stars on the ground,
While ice skaters whirl, with grace they are bound.
A penguin in pajamas slips, does a twist,
I laugh 'til I cry, oh how could I resist?

The frost bites my nose, but who cares for the chill,
When snowmen are winking, and giving a thrill.
With laughter infectious, and mirth all around,
I'm charmed by a winter that's wonderfully sound.

Laughter Beneath the Crystal Canopy

Under the branches, laughter beams,
Snowflakes dance in silly dreams.
A squirrel slips, and oh, what fun!
Hilarious antics under the sun.

Twirling around, kids take a dive,
Snowman's got swagger, feeling alive.
A snowball flies, a playful chase,
Nature's laughter fills the space.

Evergreen Dreams Beneath Whispering Snow

In green attire, the trees conspire,
Whispers of cheer, as giggles inspire.
A rabbit hops with a knowing grin,
Who knew winter could feel like a win?

Mittens mismatched, a fashion spree,
Frosty noses and merry glee.
Sliding on ice, oh what a sight,
Spreading warmth in the chilly night.

Frostbitten Grins and Treetop Whispers

Frostbitten grins, we dote in delight,
Treetops chuckle in the soft, pale light.
With snowmen who joke about their hats,
Dancing through snow, oh how time spats!

Cheerful critters join in the show,
As snowflakes flutter, feeling the flow.
Whimsical wonders in nature's glow,
Making memories wrapped in winter's throw.

The Magic of Pines in the January Dawn

Pines stretch tall, with laughs galore,
Morning light shines on winter's floor.
A blizzard of giggles fills the air,
Chasing my shadow without a care.

Snowballs whiz, the fun's on track,
Giggling elves in a frosty pack.
Season's charm with humor in flip,
A hearty chortle on winter's trip.

Snowy Canopy of Contentment

Beneath the fluffy white so bold,
Squirrels skit and scurry, oh so uncontrolled.
Flakes tickle noses, cold yet sweet,
As snowmen wobble on their twiggy feet.

Giggles echo through the winter's breath,
As laughter dances, cheating chilly death.
Hot cocoa spills on frosty paws,
Creating chaos with no sense of cause.

Threads of Laughter in Winter's Dance

A snowball flies, it finds its mark,
But then it splatters, sparks a spark.
Chasing friends through drifts of fun,
Until one slips and lands—oh, what a run!

Scarves get tangled, hats fly high,
As winter games invoke a sigh.
What's that? A bunny with a bow?
Maybe he's here to steal the show!

The Warmth of Glittering Nights

When stars twinkle on the soft white ground,
Hot chestnuts crackle, laughter's found.
Dancing shadows, flickering light,
As giggles erupt through the chilly night.

Comets slide, and wishes soar,
Who knew winter could bring so much more?
We roast marshmallows, then a sly little pine,
Whispers secrets, 'Don't cross that line!'

Frosty Kisses Beneath the Trees

Under branches wrapped with snowy flair,
Kisses exchanged, if you dare!
A blush is hidden beneath the frost,
When snowflakes tumble, love is tossed.

Icicles hang like twinkling strings,
Hearing laughter as the forest sings.
Oops! A slip on crusty snow,
Giggles bubble, and cheeks aglow!

Stars Falling on a Wintry Night

A snowman wobbles with a silly grin,
His carrot nose squished, a battle to win.
The stars above giggle, twinkling with cheer,
As I trip over snowdrifts, feeling the sneer.

The sleds take off, with a squeak and a slide,
While snowflakes dance, they take us for a ride.
With mittens on sideways and scarves loosely tied,
We'll race down the hill, with laughter as our guide.

Sunbeams Through the Icy Branches

Sunbeams peek in, through branches so bright,
A squirrel wears shades, what a marvelous sight!
With icicles dangling, like teeth from a mouth,
We bounce past the trees, swirling north to the south.

The puddles are frozen, I slip with a shout,
The sun beams down, laughing, there's no doubt.
With shadows that shimmy, and branches that sway,
We prance through the glimmer, brightening our day.

Whispers of Winter's Embrace

Whispers of winter prance on the breeze,
A penguin in slippers, roaming with ease.
With snowflakes that tickle and make us all sneeze,
We gather for snowball fights, armed with some cheese!

The cozy hot chocolate, we share with delight,
As marshmallows bounce like they're ready to fight.
Each sip is a giggle, a snort, and a cheer,
As winter weaves laughter, keeping us near.

Frosted Laughter in the Forest

In the frosted forest, critters unite,
A rabbit's got hiccups, what a silly fright!
While foxes are frolicking, spreading their cheer,
The trees are eavesdropping, they seem to hear.

With laughter erupting, echoing around,
The owls hoot back, like a comedic sound.
With snowball shenanigans, we all join the fun,
In this frosty adventure, we're never outrun!

Tinsel-Colored Hues of Winter

A squirrel slid down a branch so sleek,
In search of nuts, so bold and cheeky.
With every twist and every turn,
He tripped on snow, oh how he yearned!

The trees wear coats of shimmering white,
Pretending they're all dressed for a party tonight.
While snowmen dance with carrot noses,
They're plotting mischief, or so it poses.

Hot cocoa spills on a frosty day,
Marshmallows giggle as they sway.
Frosty lips that can't quite sip,
A sweetened slip leads to a sugary trip!

The air is crisp, the laughter loud,
Snowball fights erupt, they're feeling proud.
With every chuckle, the snowflakes swirl,
In tinsel-tinted fun, let joy unfurl!

Pine-Cloaked Merriment Under Grey Skies

A pine tree dressed in itchy garb,
Yet smiles wide, oh how it robs!
Of giggles shared beneath its shade,
As laughter dances in the glade.

A raccoon peeks with mischief planned,
But tiptoes back, it's far too grand.
The squirrels cheer with tiny glee,
Plotting tricks on wobbly knees.

Fluffy cheeks and noses bright,
Action-packed in snowy flight.
Comically tumbling, landing loud,
With pride, they bounce—oh such a crowd!

Whispers of frost in playful air,
Each snowflake giggles, light as a hair.
Beneath grey skies, hearts take flight,
A pine-cloaked wonder, pure delight!

Lush Green Against a White Canvas

A garland of greens, so bright, so bold,
Stands out in contrast to the frigid cold.
Amidst the white, a sneak peek flares,
The holiday spirit, double the cares!

A snowman's hat on a cactus rests,
Who knew such humor could manifest?
With painted rocks and twinkling eyes,
They're plotting a prank, oh what a surprise!

Socks go missing from the laundry's cheer,
But the pine trees know, they've hidden them near.
The dance of the pines through the snowflakes' twirl,
Spins stories of laughter, an evergreen whirl.

Lush green joy 'neath a frosty sky,
Silly antics cause giggles to fly.
A colorful canvas, all feel the fun,
United by laughter as bright as the sun!

Moments of Warmth in the Cold

A cat in a box, snug as a bug,
Wonders why everyone is so smug.
Paw prints lead to a pizza slice,
With giggles bounced, who rolls the dice?

Fuzzy socks and cocoa in hand,
The warmest fire in all the land.
Friends gather 'round, their breath like clouds,
A battle of wits with chuckles so loud!

Snowflakes cheekily trickle down,
While snowplows chase, all wearing a frown.
But shovelers laugh amidst the strife,
Creating snow angels—this is life!

In cozy nooks where mischief plays,
Each moment is bright, as laughter stays.
Even the cold can be quirky and bright,
As friendships flourish in sheer delight!

Whirlwind of White Beneath the Pines

Snowflakes dance like tiny sprites,
Spinning round in silly flights.
Sleds zoom past, a comical scene,
Laughter echoes where we've been.

Frosty noses, cheeks aglow,
We pretend to be fast like a snowplow.
Someone slips, lands with a thud,
We all giggle, what a dud!

Snowmen sport ridiculous hats,
With carrots for noses and fluffy mats.
A snowball fight breaks out in jest,
Who knew winter could be this blessed?

Underneath those towering trees,
We sip hot cocoa, feel the breeze.
Laughter fills the frosty air,
Playful memories, beyond compare.

Sparkling Moments in the Stillness

Twinkling lights on branches shine,
Like a squirrel with a glass of wine.
Icicles hang like chandelier bling,
Nature's laugh is what we bring.

Caught in a moment, we play in white,
Snowballs thrown with all our might.
Muffled giggles, a surprise attack,
Frosty fun keeps us on track.

Through the drifts we tumble and roll,
Finding treasures, what a goal!
A snow angel here and there,
Who knew fun could fill the air?

In these hours, so absurdly bright,
We nestle close, it feels just right.
As pine boughs sway and whisper low,
Together we bask in the winter glow.

The Lighthearted Serenade of December

Singing carols, but out of tune,
With frosty breath beneath the moon.
Each off-note makes the laughter swell,
Winter's fun, we know so well.

Gingerbread men, a tasty sight,
We decorate with sheer delight.
But one escapes, a cookie thief,
No one can find him, what a relief!

Snowy shovels become our steed,
As we ride down hills at lightning speed.
Squeals of joy as we collide,
In this winter wonderland, we glide.

Palm trees missed, but pine trees rule,
With winter games, we're feeling cool.
In this snowy bliss we adore,
Winter's antics leave us wanting more.

Icy Branches, Warm Hearts

Branches heavy with icy coats,
Snowballs fly, so let's take votes!
Whose aim is best? Who's got the skills?
Giggles echo through the hills.

Headfirst into a snowbank dive,
With our frosty friends, we thrive.
A laugh or two, then someone yells,
Is it a snowstorm? Only time tells!

Cloud of snow, someone's surprise,
Ever so sneaky, we grinningly rise.
Each flurry brightens up our day,
Join the madness, hip-hip-hooray!

In this chill, we warm our souls,
Through playful games, our heartbeats roll.
As branches sparkle in winter's light,
Love and laughter fill the night.

Glimmers Beneath the Snow

Beneath the white, a hamster rolls,
With tiny boots, he defies his goals.
A snowman winks, with a carrot nose,
His scarf unties, and off it goes!

In funny hats, the squirrels play,
Stealing nuts in a clumsy way.
With every slip on icy ground,
They burst with giggles all around!

The Enchantment of Chill

When frosty air makes noses red,
The penguins dance, their tails widespread.
They waddle fast in snowy races,
With startled looks and frozen faces!

A winter hat rolls down the street,
Chasing dogs with little feet.
They dodge and weave with joyful barks,
Creating laughter in the parks!

Pine Scented Smiles

Up in the trees, a squirrel spies,
A gingerbread house made to surprise.
He grabs a piece, then prances away,
While all his friends are in dismay!

Each pinecone rolls, a bouncing ball,
Through snowflakes that gently fall.
They laugh and chase with glee so bright,
While snowflakes dance in pure delight!

A Symphony of Frost and Cheer

A snowflake lands on a cat's nose,
She sneezes loud, and off it goes!
The neighborhood erupts in laughter,
As snowmen chase the cat thereafter!

With cocoa mugs and marshmallows tall,
The penguins swagger at the mall.
Slippery floors, oh what a sight!
Their wobbly dance brings pure delight!

The Cheerful Chill of Solstice

Frosty noses, goofy grins,
Sledding down with all our kin.
Snowflakes dance like little sprites,
Laughter echoes, pure delights.

Cocoa spills on wooly mittens,
Snowman wears our oldest kittens.
With each slip, we all just squeal,
Winter's fun, a big reveal!

Snowball fights in dizzy whirl,
Chasing friends who hike and twirl.
Every fall adds a new cheer,
Winter's mischief, oh so near!

So pack your smiles, come join the race,
In this frosty, joyful space.
We'll create a snowy show,
Chill, but always in the glow.

Winter's Heartbeat in the Woods

Snowflakes fall with gentle grace,
Tickling trees in a friendly chase.
Bushy tails and squirrel chatter,
Who knew that winter's all that matters?

Icicles glisten like long teeth,
As penguins slide, no hint of grief.
Nature's giggle fills the air,
Amusement waits everywhere!

Brrr, don't freeze your little nose,
Join the dance, as nature shows.
Hop and skip on snowy trails,
In this fun, we cannot fail!

So let's embrace the chilly thrill,
With sparkles dancing on the hill.
Every twirl, a snowy quest,
In playful winter, we are blessed.

Pine Sentries Beneath a Silver Veil

Tall and proud, the pines they stand,
Cloaked in white like nature's band.
Whispering winds, a tickled ear,
Swaying limbs in playful cheer.

Squirrels hide their treasure stashes,
While we slip and see our crashes.
Mittens lost and hats in trees,
Beneath the pines, we squeal with ease.

A cheeky fox joins in the game,
Making fun of our snowball fame.
Pines chuckle with each frosty laugh,
Nature's joy, our goofy craft!

So come along, let's dance and play,
Underneath the pines today.
With every shove and every fall,
In this winter wonderland, we all have a ball!

The Bright Side of a Snowy Scene

Puddles freeze in morning light,
Slippery steps give quite a fright.
But up we go, and down we glide,
Winter wonders, take us on a ride!

With every snowman chirping 'hi',
Mittens waving, oh, oh my!
Giggling kids on saucer slicks,
Finding joy in all the tricks.

Each snowflake tells a silly tale,
While mischief dances on the trail.
Frosty fingers, rosy cheeks,
In winter's grip, no time for leaks!

So grab a friend, let's make a fuss,
In snowy realms, it's all for us.
Through each storm and every gleam,
We'll toast to laughter; that's our theme!

Clusters of Light Amidst the Trees

Tiny bulbs are blinking bright,
In trees that dance with pure delight.
Squirrels skate on branches high,
As whispers of laughter float by.

Tinsel tangled in the boughs,
Bells ringing, oh what a rouse!
Icicles dangle like a frown,
But soon they'll wear a snowman crown.

A gingerbread army on parade,
Marching through the hoar frost glade.
With cookies perched upon their heads,
While mom and dad hide 'neath their beds.

Laughter crackles, a fizzy cheer,
As snowballs fly from far and near.
In this wonderland of white,
Every snowfall is pure delight!

Frosted Memories on the Wind

The flurries wink and swirl around,
While we make snow angels on the ground.
Hot cocoa warms our frosty hands,
As marshmallows dance like tiny bands.

Frost bites cheeks with gleeful glee,
As laughter echoes from every tree.
The snowman's nose, a carrot bright,
Is drooped over like it's seen the light.

Chasing shadows, we tumble and roll,
And find that snowball in a hole.
With hats askew and scarves in tow,
We'll conquer the world, oh, what a show!

Frosted memories spin like a top,
In this winter wonder, we'll never stop.
Each moment a treasure so sublime,
In this frosty dance, we bide our time!

A Tapestry of Lighthearted Whispers

The twinkling lights spread out like tales,
As giggles ride on laughing gales.
Pine trees wear their glittered dress,
Transforming every moment, no less!

A reindeer pranced, its antlers wide,
While elves debated how to slide.
Snowflakes flurry with silly toss,
Like candy canes that dare to floss.

Chubby cheeks from winter's zest,
Encouraging the snowmen to contest.
With each wobble, a movement grand,
As frosty whispers fill the land.

With playful winks and sprightly jigs,
The snowflakes freeze on dancing pigs.
In a swirl of fun, we lose our cares,
In this tapestry, laughter ensnares!

The Warmth of Mirth in the Cold

When cold winds blow and chill the bones,
We gather 'round, forgetting groans.
Mittens mingle with snickers bright,
As shadows chuckle in wintry light.

Snowdrifts hide the neighbor's car,
A snowball's throw can travel far!
With cheeks aglow, we take our aim,
And giggles soar, it's all a game!

Hot drinks bubble, froth in the air,
As we trade stories, laughter everywhere.
Each silly anecdote twists like a vine,
Binding us closer, oh so fine!

A snowflake falls, a tickle, a tease,
Drifting down from the frosty trees.
In this cold, our hearts stay bold,
Finding warmth where mirth takes hold!

Enchanted Trails of Pine

In the woods where shadows play,
Squirrels race, oh what a fray!
With acorns flying, laughter swells,
Nature's circus, oh, it tells!

Snowflakes tickle, what a sight,
Snowmen wobble, left and right!
A bunny hops, it trips and slips,
With comic timing, laughter grips!

Pine trees stand in silent glee,
While birds in boots sing merrily.
A gust of wind, a hat takes flight,
Chasing it brings pure delight!

The trail ends with a cheerful cheer,
As snowflakes dance, oh so near!
In the woods, the fun won't cease,
Each step brings laughter, piece by piece!

A Canvas of Cheer in the Cold

Upon the canvas, snowflakes swirl,
A painter's mishap, what a twirl!
Brushes made of pine and ice,
Creating giggles, oh so nice!

The snowman dons a wobbly hat,
With eyes of buttons, looking flat.
A carrot nose that's slightly bent,
His jolly smile is heaven-sent!

Kids in mittens make a mess,
Snowballs flying, more or less.
With each throw, a fit of glee,
Artistry in laughter, can't you see?

As day winds down, the chill sets in,
But merry moments always win!
On this canvas, fun's the goal,
Creating memories, heart and soul!

Whispers of Light in the Frost

In frosty woods, the air so bright,
Laughter echoes, pure delight.
A snowflake lands on a pup's nose,
He sneezes loud, oh how it goes!

Branches groan with snowy bliss,
While woodland critters share a kiss.
A bear with shades, he takes a stroll,
Dancing twigs, oh what a role!

The night ignites with twinkling stars,
Riding sleighs, we dodge the cars.
With cheeks so rosy and laughter free,
This frosty fun is pure esprit!

As whispers light the chilly air,
We gather round without a care.
In the frosty glow, we share a grin,
Each moment cherished, let's begin!

The Frosted Dance of Cheer

Snowflakes spin in frosty flair,
As we dance without a care.
With flailing arms and silly feet,
We glide and twirl, oh what a treat!

Nutty squirrels join the show,
Dressed in scarves, they steal the glow.
With wiggly tails and giggles loud,
The forest spirits feel so proud!

Here comes a rabbit, side to side,
With snowball hops, oh what a ride!
A frosted party, we shout hooray,
In winter's arms, we laugh and play!

As night descends, the moon does beam,
Illuminating our joyful dream.
In a dance of laughter, hands entwined,
Frosty fun, our hearts aligned!

Twinkling Lights on Frosty Branches

On branches draped like candy canes,
Twinkling bulbs drive squirrels insane.
They dance and leap, part of the show,
While birds wear sweaters, don't you know?

A snowman winks with a carrot nose,
He tells bad jokes, as laughter grows.
Pine scent mingles with cocoa cheer,
Who knew winter could bring such a year?

Frosty fingers grip the hot mug tight,
As snowflakes swirl in twinkling flight.
The cat gets stuck in the Christmas tree,
While Grandma sips tea and squawks with glee.

Out comes the twirl and slip on ice,
Giggles erupt, and oh, how nice!
We sing and dance like reindeer overhead,
In this snowy circus, we laugh instead!

Enchantment in the Icy Air

In the frosty air, a snowball fight,
We hurl with glee until it's night.
Slipping, sliding, a winter ballet,
With noses red, we're here to play!

The snowflakes twinkle like tiny stars,
Each soft landing, a giggle spar.
Penguins prance, and so do we,
Chasing each other with pure glee.

With a whistle here and a toboggan there,
We zoom down hills, wind in our hair.
No one escapes the laughter spree,
As we tumble down, just wait and see!

The frosty air brings silly grins,
With each playful shove, the fun begins.
We squeal and laugh, not a single care,
In this winter wonderland, magic is rare!

Sledding Down Memory Lane

Grabbing sleds, we race from heights,
Down we zoom, amid squeals and sights.
Like giant ducks on slippery slopes,
We're flying high, fueled by our hopes.

Frosty cheeks and snow-filled hats,
We tumble down like chubby cats.
Each crash is met with raucous cheers,
As we build memories that last for years.

Snowmen watching from their snowy throne,
Together we giggle, never alone.
A face-plant here, a tumble there,
But oh, the laughter fills the air!

As the sun sets, our cheeks alight,
With stories told in fading light.
Sledding down, like time on a reel,
Who needs a warm blanket? We've got zeal!

Silent Lullabies in the Snow

Under blankets of snow, we drift so light,
Whispers of winter, soft and bright.
The snowflakes swirl in a dizzy dance,
As dreams take flight, a snowy romance.

A squirrel snoozes on a fluffy mound,
While winter's choir sings all around.
Pinecones yawn with a crackling sleep,
As the world outside begins to creep.

Frosty winks and chilly sighs,
Snowball fights and surprise pies!
The moon peeks in with a mischievous glare,
In this hush, we find moments to share.

With each breath, a frosty puff,
We melt into laughter — never enough!
The silence holds secrets of snowmen's glee,
In this winter lullaby, come sing with me!

Glacial Lullabies of Contentment

A penguin slides on icy sprawl,
He bumps a tree, just like a ball.
The snowflakes giggle, swirl in flight,
As chubby squirrels dance in delight.

Frosty air tickles noses bright,
A snowman's hat takes off in flight.
Be careful, dear, the sled's too fast,
We'll crash in laughter, what a blast!

The winter sun peeks through the frost,
A bunny hops, oh, not a lost!
With flapping ears that tease the chill,
He leaps and lands on oodles of thrill.

So raise a mug of cocoa warm,
As snowflakes weave a silly charm.
In frozen fun, we'll find our cheer,
A giggly dance, with friends so near.

Pitch Pine Glow in the Darkness

At dusk the lights begin to twinkle,
A pine tree's glow makes spirits crinkle.
With candy canes and laughter near,
Those sneaky squirrels bring holiday cheer.

A raccoon strains to reach the top,
He tips the tree, and down they plop!
With giggles echoing through the woods,
The furry friends mix like hot goods.

The shadows play a friendly game,
As pine cones fall like snowflakes' fame.
A snowman's nose, oh, what a sight,
A carrot thief takes off in flight!

Let's gather 'round the glowing wreathe,
With silly stories, there's never a sheath.
In laughter's warmth, we'll always huddle,
As pitch pine ignites our wintry cuddle.

The Magic Beneath Winter's Glistening

Underneath the sparkling sky,
A chubby chipmunk gives a sigh.
He lost his stash, oh what a mess!
In his search, he finds a new dress!

Snowflakes fall, a fluffy shower,
A snowball flies—a snowy flower.
With giggles fluttering through the air,
The winter sprites dance everywhere.

A fluffy bunny hops so bold,
He dashes in the world of cold.
The twinkling stars are laughs galore,
As frosty friends join in the score!

Let's stack some snow in towers high,
With carrot eyes and a tilt to the sky.
In every flake, a wish is spun,
In winter's heart, we share the fun.

Delights in the Drifting Snow

Snowflakes twirl, like dreams on wing,
Silly thoughts of winter's fling.
A cat in boots prances with style,
While squirrels munch and watch a while.

The snowy path is fun to trace,
With steaming mugs, we find our space.
A snowman's nose, a bit askew,
Encouraging laughs from me to you.

The frosty trees chuckle low,
As the wind tries a cheeky blow.
With every flake, a story spins,
As laughter echoes where joy begins.

Let's tumble through the drifts of white,
And build a fort for silly fights.
In drifting snow, we'll create a show,
With hearts so light, let the laughter flow!

Pine Boughs Adrift in Laughter

In a forest thick, with branches wide,
A squirrel slipped, what a wild ride!
He tangled in needles, then did a twirl,
While the woodland critters all gave a whirl.

The birds chuckled loud, perched high in the trees,
As squirrels danced under, with snowflakes that tease.
With every leap and a giggle-filled sound,
They frolicked about, in the snow all around.

Pine cones were flying, oh what a sight!
The fluffy white snow just added delight.
While raccoons snickered, with mischief in mind,
In this cotton candy world, humor they'd find.

As branches did shimmy, and laughter did swell,
In the heart of the woods, all was funny and swell.
Nature's own carnival, laughter the theme,
In a winter wonder, where humor does beam.

Frost and Merriment

In where the snowflakes fall,
 ......ed his tail, then rolled with a ball.
But the ball was a snowman, a soft fluffy treat,
They both ended up in a snowy defeat!

The baker laughed loud, with flour on his nose,
As he slipped on a roll that went flying in throws.
A pie took a tumble, too quick to save,
While everyone gathered, their sides all did wave.

Children in mittens, with cheeks like bright roses,
Made snow angels shapes, with bright, shiny poses.
While a snowball flew past, and knocked off a hat,
And everyone cheered, "Now, isn't that brat?"

In a swirl of delight, on the ice, they would skate,
With giggles and laughter, oh, what a fate!
A tale full of frost, yet warm in our hearts,
As the joy of the season, in shady fun, starts.

Winter's Embrace and Heartfelt Grins

In the chill of the dusk, with a smile so bright,
A snowman danced wildly, just catching some light.
He twirled and he wobbled, then slipped on a patch,
The kids rolled with laughter, 'twas quite the great match!

Fluffy white pillows floated down from the skies,
Tickling the noses and covering eyes.
As mom sent them out, in jackets too tight,
They waddled like penguins, a hilarious sight!

With hot cocoa brewing, an endearing delight,
They spilled on the floor, what a comical fright!
With marshmallows bouncing, like tiny snowballs,
They giggled and cheered, in warm, cozy halls.

So let's raise a toast to the frosty, fun days,
Where laughter and warmth, in myriad ways,
Bring hearts together, with each wintry spin,
In this laughter-filled season, where grins always win.

The Shimmer of Snow-Blanketed Joy

The snow glistened bright, like diamonds galore,
While penguins in hats danced right out of the floor.
They slipped on the ice with a wiggle and swirl,
In their waddling world, oh, how they would twirl!

A little girl giggled, her cheeks all aglow,
As her puppy went bounding through soft, powdery snow.

With one mighty leap, he landed headfirst,
And the laughter erupted; oh, what a burst!

A snowball fight launched, in laughter's embrace,
With each throw and catch, it was all a mad race.
"Did that hit you or not?" they would gleefully shout,
While the parents just smiled, joining in on the bout!

As the sun set down, painting the night,
Warm hugs and bright smiles filled hearts with pure light.

With each memory crafted, under moon's soft glow,
There's magic in laughter, in snow, hearts will grow.

Milton Keynes UK
Ingram Content Group UK Ltd.
UKHW021349011224
451618UK00023B/229

9 789916 908907